T0121339

IT'S OK TO
CLIMB OUT
OF YOUR
Family
TREE

DAKODA WEST

BALBOA.
PRESS
A DIVISION OF HAY HOUSE

Balboa Press books may be ordered through booksellers or by contacting:

Balboa Press
A Division of Hay House
1663 Liberty Drive
Bloomington, IN 47403
www.balboapress.com
1 (877) 407-4847

Print information available on the last page.

ISBN: 978-1-5043-7567-2 (sc)
ISBN: 978-1-5043-7568-9 (e)

Balboa Press rev. date: 03/09/2017

This book is dedicated to

MY FAMILY

I love each and every one of you
and thank you for enriching my life in your own special way.

Table of Contents

Chapter One

It is February in Victoria and the snowdrops are heralding Spring. The sun is making an appearance after the long wet grey months. Winter lethargy is giving way to the irresistible impulse of the season.

I seemed drawn to my computer to write and share this story.

I love the title I chose for this book and believe that a majority of readers can relate to it.

This narrative is about my two individual cousins from the same family tree who found it necessary to make the climb out. It is also about me, Stephen who learned how to find freedom from both my cousin's stories.

These cousins shared their experiences with me and I feel compelled to share them with you so you know that you're not alone in your family dynamics.

I am alive!!! I feel as though I am finally free to be me.
Born to be....

I'm amazed by how much creative and productive energy is available when you are freed from reactions to anger and fear.

But, my life has not always felt like this...

I believe that we all die a little when we are sacrificing ourselves on the altar of needing to be accepted.

My death came from me not living out my own dreams and aspirations,

But instead - by living to please my family and the people I surrounded myself with.

The concept of me – physically climbing out of my family tree
– jeans, plaid shirt, ball cap, climbing boots and all –
got my adrenaline pumping.

My personality and attitude towards others is such that I don't like to intentionally harm or offend people – so how do I manage this feat?

Chapter Two

When the seed for a tree is planted or scattered about and sprouts out of the earth, all the little roots are scrambling for a sense of security.

The first life stage a tree goes through is infancy, just like you and me.

During this phase, trees are at their most vulnerable. Trees are very thin and small, though some may quickly grow taller than the average person.

Infant trees will often survive just fine on their own, but with coaxing, loving care, and attention, infant trees can grow strong and tall.

The second stage a tree goes through in its life is youth. Trees in this "teenage" phase, have long, slender branches, and pointed tops.

At this stage, their growth and form can be influenced, but their small size makes them easy to damage or kill with thoughtless action. When they are kept uninjured and free to grow, they respond with quick healthy growth.

Stage three is next: the tree's prime of life. Trees in their prime have full, round-topped crowns, filled with long, strong branches.

Now is the time to sit back and enjoy your tree. Trees in their prime of life will take care of themselves with little outside help.

The fourth phase in a tree's life is middle-age. Their crowns will flatten out as limbs grow thicker and will begin to develop their own unique character.

Trees become seniors at stage five. Senior trees have flat-topped canopies of heavy limbs, sometimes covered in short sprouts. Gaps start appearing in the canopy as the major limb systems start dying out.

At the end of their life, trees reach their twilight, stage six. Large limbs die and break off, leaving a small crown of scattered large limbs and short twigs.

All trees will inevitably die at some point, and rest in peace.

A dead tree can provide a good habitat for wildlife, providing food and shelter.

Chapter Three

I have a cousin Billy (tree stage three) who did manage secretly to climb out of his/our family tree – unnoticed – that is until his Memorial Service.

Ironically, Billy devoted five years of his life travelling and meeting as many of our relatives as he could and researching our roots.

He came up with a complex diagram dating back to 1870, which he shared with the rest of our family.

Billy's Dad and my Mom were brother and sister and we spent considerable time together as children growing up. Billy was the youngest of three children born to his parents.

To look at him he was just another ordinary guy. A little smaller than me with an average build and a good crop of dark brown hair. Thankfully good hair seems prevalent in our family.

Billy was funny and fun to be with. The life of any party. I would say now in retrospect that he was somewhat exocentric and charismatic – even as a child.

I always enjoyed Billy's visits and numerous stories – which I felt were slightly embellished - about several of our relatives and members of our extended family tree whom he had met during his travels.

I regret that I have not yet connected with our family relatives who live in the United States and beyond. We do come from a very interesting extended family

– according to Billy – embellished or not....

We have a great Aunt Maude who murdered her husband's lover by stabbing her in the back, and who shared a jail with a couple of our second Uncles, who were inmates arrested for robbery and drug related crimes.

We have Mormons, Protestants, Catholics and Jews, Democrats and Republicans. Apparently our extended family is comprised of members from all walks of life including politicians, doctors, priests and beggars – the full gambit from one extreme to the other.

Our immediate family, to my knowledge, consist of fairly traditional, honest, religious and upright citizens. However, after hearing Billy's story I may have to rethink my assumptions and judgement of character.

In his early fifties, Billy was found dead in his apartment and a memorial date, time and place was set. Billy's brother, cousin Frank, arranged for a small family service at a Funeral Chapel in Winnipeg, Manitoba.

The set time was 10:30 am on an extremely cold and snowy January morning with temperatures in the minus thirty below zero range.

I couldn't believe that the morning would be a good time to hold his service as there were many of us that had to travel from afar to attend.

However, I made it.

My family gathered in a lunch room adjacent to the Chapel, and as we were catching up with each other and setting out pictures and memories of Billy – we were asked by a rather imposing man who was dressed in black, to vacate the room and move across the hall. In this small room, we all held hands and said a short prayer before opening the door about 10 minutes later and entered into the corridor leading to the Chapel.

As soon as the door was ajar and we left the intimate prayer room, we were literally being pushed and somewhat held back by a huge crowd of strange people.

There wasn't a single familiar face in the crowd.

I whispered to another cousin Jack that it was strange that more than one Memorial service was scheduled for the same time, simply assuming that only our family would be there for Billy.

As our family took our places in the front pews of the Chapel, realization started to dawn on most of us - that all these hundreds of strangers were here to pay tribute and their last respects to 'our Billy'.

The reason we had been asked to move was so the reception room could be opened up to accommodate the overflowing crowd.

Billy's brother, cousin Frank, acting as the master of ceremonies was visibly overwhelmed by the crowd. Having being trained in the Mormon faith and public speaking, he quickly composed himself and welcomed everyone.

Billy's sister, cousin Charlotte was called on to give the eulogy on behalf of her brother.

Charlotte spoke of the Billy that the family believed they knew and loved, the kind, funny and well travelled, interesting man – who - as the service continued, it turned out bore absolutely no resemblance whatever to 'our Billy', the man whose ashes were sitting in the urn - set on the alter before us.

Next speaker was a representative from the Federal Government. It turned out that part of the crowd gathered on the right side pews sitting directly across from us, were Billy's cohorts and representatives of our Government.

I had always believed that Billy was a general clerk - but was I mistaken. From the various speeches, it turned out that Billy had attained a fair degree of prestige and was a highly regarded government employee who had published several policy papers and was extremely respected and well liked.

After several accolades, the...next speaker was from the Jewish Community. I should have realized this by all the black skull caps worn by the strangers in the back half of the Chapel. A **kippah** is a brimless cap, usually made of cloth, worn by the Jews to fulfill the customary requirement held by orthodox halachic authorities that the head be covered at all times. It is usually worn by men. Apparently most synagogues and Jewish funeral services keep a ready supply of *kippot* for the temporary use of visitors who have not brought a kippah (skull cap).

Billy, having been born & baptized a Mormon, had now been converted and received into the Jewish faith.

Thank God our convert's mother, Aunt Lois, seated in the front row of the Chapel is deaf and the dear old soul sat there bravely with a thin little smile on her face.

None of us in our family had any inkling that Billy had done this and that he was until his death, a practicing Jew.

Another revelation –

The next speaker Walter was from the Gay Community. He shared several funny stories about Billy - the one I liked the most was that Billy was a great cook and loved to entertain dinner guests. He prepared impressive gourmet meals and would greet this guests at the door clad in a tall white chief hat and an apron.

It was when he turned around that he was otherwise in the buff...

Apparently, Billy was famous for his "fruitcake" and several loaves were found in his freezer and would be served today at the reception to follow.

Next speaker was from the Musical Theatre.

Unannounced to any of his family Billy was a talented song and dance man. He was quite famous for his starring role in Johnny Appleseed where he received many acclimations.

It clearly was no surprise that the family members didn't know most of the people attending Billy's memorial service.

After the last exposé, Brother Frank - managed to regain his composure - the fallen jaws and open mouths of the relatives closed –and-

Billy was left with the afterglow of his life.

I don't condone Billy's life style; however, I do admire him for being his own person.

I think that this story could be made into a great stage play....something to consider!!

Billy's story is that he accomplished his climb out of our family tree unnoticed. However, this imposter life Billy led was not an easy burden for him to carry – and eventually the deception and frustrations caused him to take his own life.

Chapter Four

Now you know the real Billy, it is time to meet my cousin Sophie. Sophie was born in a small seaside village of around 12,000 people in New Brunswick, and is the youngest of three children born to a single mom. Sophie would be in stage four of our tree years.

Sophie's mom was married, but her husband never returned from the war, so the girls were brought up without the influence of a man. The reason I point this fact out is to give you an understanding of how Sophie was raised. There was seldom a harsh word spoken in her family and very little arguing or fighting.

Thus, Sophie never really learned how to defend herself verbally or physically.

I can still remember Sophie as being cute, with long blond curly hair, large dimples on each side of her cheek and an infectious laugh.

She made friends easily and was popular with members of the opposite sex.

Sophie was a people pleaser and wouldn't hurt a fly.

The quality of her personality to defend herself was never needed until after her Mother Heather died and she was exposed to harsh and hurtful words spoken by her siblings.

There was huge animosity regarding her right to be the executor and inheritor in their Mother's Last Will and Testament.

Sophie being the youngest in the immediate family, her older sisters automatically assumed that they would be the decision makers for their Mothers Estate.

Wrong – Mother named Sophie as her executor.

Sophie was given everything – The Power of Attorney, she was named jointly on all bank accounts, and entrusted with the Will stating that her monetary assets be split three ways with her daughters and a list of her Mother's personal and cherished items to be distributed to her sisters, grandchildren and great grandchildren following her death.

I love my cousin Sophie; we have always been close friends. Our Mothers were sisters and as children we spent many summer holidays together and have always had a deep bond.

I was always like an older brother to Sophie and she confided in me about how very hurt she was by her sisters, and how deeply grieved she was by her Mother's death.

– Heather White (1913-2012)

"Those we love must one day pass

Beyond our present sight;

To leave us, and the world we know

Without their radiant light.

But we know that like a candle,

Their lovely light will shine,

To brighten up another place,

More perfect, more divine."

Author unknown

Sophie thought she was prepared for her Mother's transition –Her mother had lived a long and healthy life and would have been 100 yrs old – and actually was, if you count her time spent in her mother's womb - when she took her last breath.

But she wasn't prepared... Sophie's Mother's death was her most difficult challenge. The grief, both emotionally and spiritually produced in her a sorrow which could not be shared - one she had to borne alone.

Her Mother had tried her upmost to raise her daughters up to be ladies and to love one another.

My dear Aunt Heather would have been so very disappointed that her death ultimately separated her family.

Sophie' sister Margaret didn't even attend the funeral. Also absent were three grandchildren and three great grandchildren who were all left money from Aunt Heather's estate so they could attend her tribute.

Dorothy is four years older than Sophie – and like cousin Billy had already left the family tree. She refuses to believe that she could belong to such a dysfunctional family.

Dot left her branch in the tree, but that is all. No touchy/feely feelings.

I hope that Dorothy will find happiness.

Margaret is still clutching the tree remembering how much she did for Sophie when she was young. There is a ten year difference in their ages, and in all fairness, Margaret did have a lot of extra responsibility taking care of Dot and Sophie while they were growing up, because Aunt Heather worked long hours as a bookkeeper.

I suspect the rationale behind my Aunt choosing Sophie to complete her affairs was perhaps because she was the daughter with the business head.

Dot is very creative and artistic and off in her own world ...and, Margaret is domineering and controlling with the best of intentions. These elder sisters questioned Sophie's integrity which she confided to me, hurt her the most.

No one takes kindly to having their honesty questioned – especially if they are innocent and the acquisitions come from your own blood and loved ones..

Both Dot and Margaret felt that Sophie had somehow managed to force their Mother into choosing her as executor of the estate.

I have heard numerous stories about families torn apart by money – but was naive enough to think – surely not in our family.

With the animosity expressed by her sisters, Sophie chose to climb out of her family tree – not caring if her decent was noticed or not. It was only through telling her story that she was able to heal herself and to carry on. Fortunately our loved ones stay with us in our ongoing life stories

There is not a person in your life who isn't here to teach you something about yourself

(Writer, Kristine Carlson)

Let's pierce through the muck and go direct to emotions.

Family dynamics can affect everyone – young and old. I've even heard stories about parents who often want to climb away from their offspring for reasons of vast disappointment, disillusionment, and frustration. These emotions are not confined and are multi-generational.

Some of you will have your own stories to write or tell.

What is important is that you do express yourself in order for healing to occur.

So, how do we climb out of our family tree - alive?

Unnoticed?

Chapter Five

Stephen's story (stage five of the tree)

Most of us are spoiled by hard working parents whose goal it was to provide "everything" to and for us.

In many homes, both parents worked and were too tired at the end of the day to discipline their children or face confrontation – or took a different approach and were hard disciplinarians. Either way, most children grew up to be independent.

But not me. My mother stayed home –Dad was gone working most of the time, but spent quality time with me when he could. We had numerous family vacations which were great times.

My Dad came here as an immigrant at the age of ten with his Father, Mother, two sisters and a brother and the grand total of $40.00 amongst them. In Dad's day there were no freebies or Prime Minister to greet them, resulting in him believing that hard work was the only way to make it in this world.

Dad tried to pass down his ethics to me, but I am not him and I have very different views of life. But, because of my nurturing, loving Mother I did not become independent. I wanted to please my parents. This is not to say that most young people don't want to be people pleasers, but many prefer to please themselves, then the parents.

I have been gifted with a clever mind and spend countless hours dreaming up inventions and ways to help mankind. Never giving up on my dreams.

Sure I work to make a living – but my work wasn't fulfilling –

I always wanted to be an astronaut. In my opinion there isn't anything more beautiful than viewing the galaxies.

I believe in God, but am more spiritual than traditional. Attending Church is not something I do except when visiting with my family at Christmas or Easter.

Even though I've made the climb – I haven't lost respect for my family.

Turning thirty, I also became more independent. I decided to make my own climb away from my family because of the immense differences in our thinking.

OK, so now I have made a choice to distance myself

from my family. –

what next?

I had much to learn from Sophie about the nature of opposition. I needed to be prepared for the bangs and bruises headed my way from my family. I feel so sad realizing that I am expected to pay for a debt I never owed.

To help you avoid unkind feedback from your family – please remember that this is your very own personal climb. You don't need to say anything to anybody and you don't need to be like all the other leaves in the family tree.

You don't stop loving your family – you just stop being accountable to them. Once awareness becomes obvious, believe me; families don't take kindly to this, but in time I trust that they will have more respect for me.

I have a new confidence in myself.

Quote: We are never prepared for life – that is what makes it worth living– the spontaneity, the constant changes, our personal growth. Mark Twain

Chapter Six

The "Tools" I used to make the climb were:

To become really aware of my thoughts and present attitude, to ponder, meditate and plan – just small steps –

This conditioning I had - has taken me years to develop and will undoubtedly take years to undo. –

I kept telling myself start, – don't procrastinate – begin today.

Change your thoughts – Change your life.. book written by Dr. Wayne Dyer was my first reference. Best-selling author and lecturer Wayne W. Dyer described the steps necessary to help me eliminate my self-doubt, and to discover how my thoughts can change my life, and helped me find true happiness.

> I kept working on the realization that my thoughts are drawn through magnetic vibrations towards other thought streams, positive or negative.

I kept constantly reminding myself that I had to control my thoughts. Change isn't easy, but of course you can do it if you know it is worth it. Dr. Dyer said "as you think so shall you become."

I must confess that controlling my thoughts was a huge challenge for me. Your mind is where you process all of your experiences and relationships.

I wrote my goal down and referred to it often – It is good to have a goal – but also wise to set a date for completion. I was programmed for the past forty years and all this cannot be erased immediately.

For me, working daily on my thoughts – took almost a year – before I gained the confidence I needed to believe in me and only me.

Chapter Seven

Most of us use the Law of Attraction (LOA) in our everyday lives, ... but the "Big Secret" is most people do not realize it. So they miss out on how to use it deliberately to create whatever they want and desire.

After learning and studying the law of attraction, my life clearly changed for the better. We all tend to slip back into our most practiced ways of thinking from time to time, especially when we are in the vicinity of negative people or in a negative circumstance.

But, I have learned several ways to help me stay in that positive train of thought from being conscious of the Law of Attraction - and it has been amazing.

My life is much more peaceful and happy, because I now realize that I am the attractor of my own life experiences.

In the book *THE SECRET* Jack Canfield wrote:

"Decide what you want. Believe you can have it. Believe you deserve it and believe it is possible for you. And then close your eyes every day for several minutes and visualize having what you already want, feeling the feelings of already having it. Come out of that and focus on what you're grateful for already, and really enjoy it.

Then go into your day and release it to the Universe and trust that the Universe will figure out how to manifest it".

The law of attraction states that every positive or negative event that happened with you was attracted to you. There are really only three basic steps: ask, believe, and receive.

Be sure about what you want and when you do decide please don't doubt yourself. Remember that you're sending a request to the Universe which is created by thoughts and therefore responds to thoughts.

Know exactly what it is that you want.

If you're not definite, the Universe will get an unclear frequency and will send you unwanted results. So be sure it is something you have strong passion for.

Ask the Universe for it.

Make your request. See it in your mind and send a picture of what you want to the Universe. The Universe will answer. See this thing as already yours.

Write your wish down. Begin with "I am so happy and grateful now that..." and complete the sentence telling the Universe what it is that you want. Write it in the present tense as if you have it right now.

Feel it. Feel the way you will now after receiving your wish.

It is important for you to act, speak, and think as if you are receiving it now. This is actually the most important, powerful step in using the Law of Attraction because this is where it starts working!

Therefore, the universe will manifest this thought and feeling, and you will receive it.

Show gratitude. Write down all the things the Universe has given you. Being thankful will motivate the Universe to do even more things and will draw more things into your life.

Mind Calming.

For me, I prefer to be alone. I like the room to be dark. The room should also be relatively quiet. Comfort is most important. I sit in my favourite chair or lie down on my bed and take deep breaths to calm my mind. After becoming totally relaxed, I allow my mind to ponder the specific changes I want to occur in my personality and habits.

I see myself going about my daily life as the person I want to be doing the things I want to do. With your visualization still fresh in your mind, capture whatever images, symbols, thoughts, concepts or ideas that came up for you. You can use words, drawings, stick figures or color to capture a particular feeling.

By learning how to control my thoughts and attract what I want, I was able to move past breakups, issues at work and overcome money and family problems.

I simply live in the NOW. Not in the past or the future, but instead I focus on this very moment – what is happening to me and how I am reacting. I can, by using this method of NOW, have power over and move through the majority of uneasy situations using them to my advantage and I have achieved success.

I pasted a note near my phone so that when family members

called –

I was reminded not to let anything derogatory that family may say to me - penetrate. It is like putting an imaginary bubble around yourself that words can't break through.

This idea helped me immensely.

It was my game to play and family members were not invited by me to play.

Chapter Eight

It is ok to climb up, down and out of the family tree.

This is not to say that you no longer love your family –

it is for us to realize that we are part of a much greater family.

I had tried so hard in vain to please my family. I had to climb out of our family tree as I felt blinded by the leaves and branches and had to look at the tree from the outside before I could climb back into my family tree – with a much deeper appreciation for the people I love.

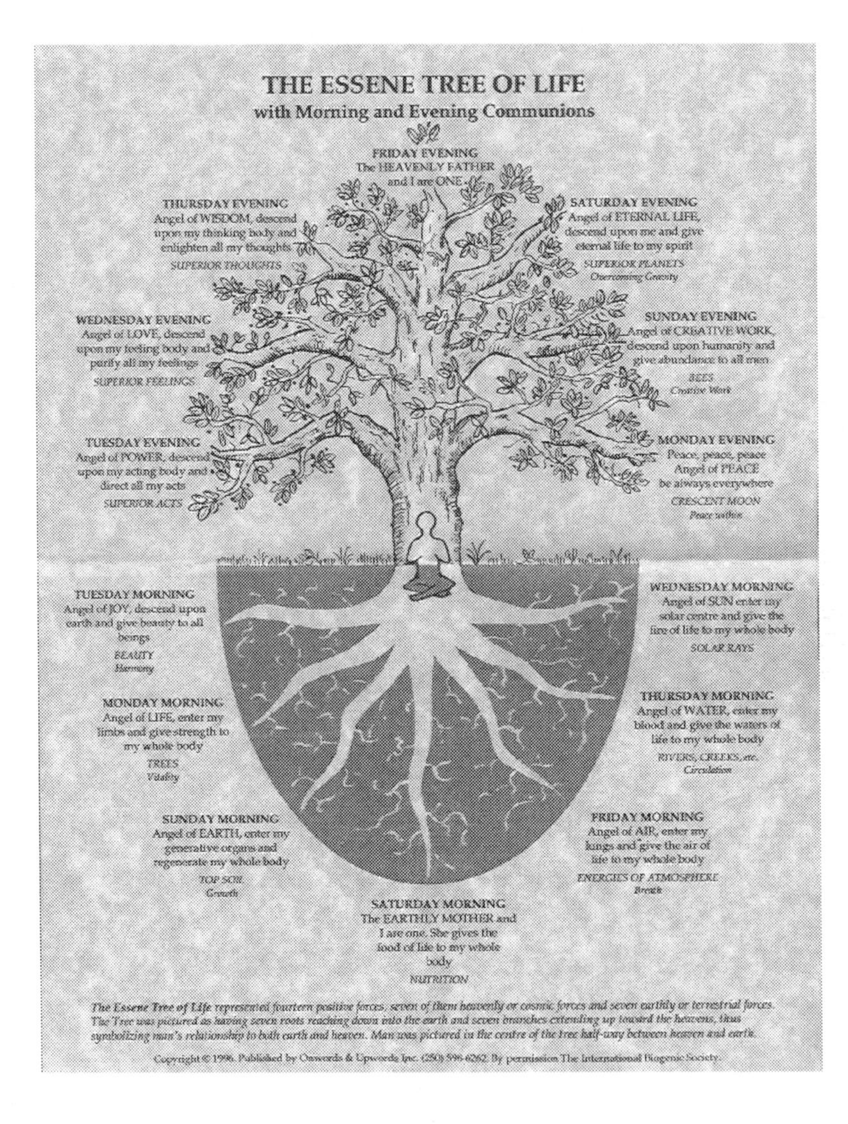

THE ESSENE TREE OF LIFE
with Morning and Evening Communions
FRIDAY EVENING
The HEAVENLY FATHER and I are ONE
THURSDAY EVENING
Angel of WISDOM, descend upon my thinking body and enlighten all my thoughts
SUPERIOR THOUGHTS
SATURDAY EVENING
Angel of ETERNAL LIFE, descend upon me and give eternal life to my spirit
SUPERIOR PLANETS
Overcoming Gravity
WEDNESDAY EVENING
Angel of LOVE, descend upon my feeling body and purify all my feelings
SUPERIOR FEELINGS
SUNDAY EVENING
Angel of CREATIVE WORK, descend upon humanity and give abundance to all men
BEES
Creative Work
TUESDAY EVENING
Angel of POWER, descend upon my acting body and direct all my acts
SUPERIOR ACTS
MONDAY EVENING
Peace, peace, peace
Angel of PEACE
be always everywhere
CRESCENT MOON
Peace within
TUESDAY MORNING
Angel of JOY, descend upon earth and give beauty to all beings
BEAUTY
Harmony
WEDNESDAY MORNING
Angel of SUN enter my solar centre and give the fire of life to my whole body
SOLAR RAYS
MONDAY MORNING
Angel of LIFE, enter my limbs and give strength to my whole body
TREES
Vitality
THURSDAY MORNING
Angel of WATER, enter my blood and give the waters of life to my whole body
RIVERS, CREEKS, etc.
Circulation
SUNDAY MORNING
Angel of EARTH, enter my generative organs and regenerate my whole body
TOP SOIL
Growth
FRIDAY MORNING
Angel of AIR, enter my lungs and give the air of life to my whole body
ENERGIES OF ATMOSPHERE
Breath
SATURDAY MORNING
The EARTHLY MOTHER and I are one. She gives the food of life to my whole body
NUTRITION
The Essene Tree of Life represented fourteen positive forces, seven of them heavenly or cosmic forces and seven earthly or terrestrial forces. The Tree was pictured as having seven roots reaching down into the earth and seven branches extending up toward the heavens, thus symbolizing man's relationship to both earth and heaven. Man was pictured in the centre of the tree half-way between heaven and earth.
Copyright © 1996. Published by Onwords & Upwords Inc. (250) 598-6262. By permission The International Biogenic Society.

Ravinic literature is replete with the imagery of the tree, its symbolism and its significance. The Torah is referred to as the "Tree of Life" and, mankind, likewise, has been compared to the tree.

"Man is an upside-down tree, for a tree's roots are in the ground below, while man's roots are above – for a tree's sustenance is from the ground while man's sustenance is from Heaven."

The Essene Tree of Life shows our relationship with all the heavenly and earthly forces. The ancient and timeless Essene teachings are as applicable today as they were 2000 years ago.

Spiritual development –

Life is not about what you have accomplished or accumulated in your life – it is who you are.

Look in the mirror – take a good deep look and don't whatever you do be harsh on yourself. Love you. Live your life accordingly so that others will love you too.

God has unconditional love for you – you need unconditional love for you.

My wish is that you will join me as we journey through life together by accepting who you are, and not feel that you owe your family tree descendents anything more than your love.

Love never fails. May you experience love and joy for your entire existence.

The Higher Self

Love is not possessive.

To love is to give; love is a radiation,

a sending forth from the heart of a sweet essence which heals.

from The White Eagle Lodge

References

The White Eagle Publishing Trust

The Secret – by – Rhonda Byrne

Real Magic – by - Dr. Wayne Dyer

Excuses Begone by Dr. Wayne Dyer

Change Your Thoughts – by -Dr. Wayne Dyer

Onwords & Upwords Publishers

Printed in the United States
By Bookmasters